Tarot

JONATHAN DEE

This is a Parragon Book
This edition published in 2003

Parragon
Queen Street House
4 Queen Street
Bath BA1 1HE, UK

ISBN: 1-40541-114-7

A copy of the CIP data for this book is available from the British Library upon
request.

The right of Louis Canasta to be identified as the author of this work has been
asserted in accordance with Section 77 of the Copyright, Designs and Patents Act
of 1988.

Editorial, design and layout by Essential Books.

Printed and bound in China

Contents

First Steps

WHAT ARE TAROT CARDS?

There are many types of fortune-telling cards on the market these days, but not all of them are Tarot cards.

The Tarot is a specialized set of cards that has a very long history. Some have even claimed that they derive from the ancient Egyptian civilization, but I think it more likely that they are European in origin and date from various mystical traditions some time around the period of the Crusades.

A Tarot deck is similar to an ordinary pack of playing cards. Both have four suits numbered from ace to ten. In a Tarot deck these are known as the Minor Arcana, and instead of Clubs, Hearts, Spades and Diamonds, the Tarot suits are Wands, Cups, Swords and Pentacles.

Unlike an ordinary pack of cards, each suit has four court cards rather than three: King, Queen, Knight and Page, making fifty-six cards in the Minor Arcana.

In addition to the Minor cards, the Tarot deck has twenty-two 'extra', cards known as the Major Arcana. These do not belong to any suit, but have their own numbers (with the exception of the Fool), a symbolic image and a title.

If, when doing a reading, more Minor cards occur than Major, then your destiny is mostly in your hands. If it is the other way around, fate governs your future.

The following sections of the book deal with the meanings of individual cards, as well as possible combinations and how to lay them out to create a reading. Each interpretation is divided into upright and reversed meanings showing the positive and negative effects of the cards. However, it is permissible to use only the upright interpretations if you think that the reversed ones are too hard for the beginner.

HOW TO START

The first rule is to become familiar with your cards. Get to know the pictures, shuffle them a lot, carry them about with you, even sleep with them by your bed so they absorb your personal energies and become uniquely yours.

Many Tarot experts recommend keeping the cards wrapped in black silk and/or in a wooden box. I keep mine in a blue silk bag, and I know other readers who just keep them in a drawer. The important thing to remember is that the cards are yours alone, and should be special to you.

You should not allow others to play with the cards or even pick them up without your permission. Most certainly you should not allow anyone else to read them.

Once you have begun the process of making your pack of Tarot cards individual to you, you can start to practise reading them.

The Major Arcana

THE FOOL

Unnumbered
Ruled by Uranus and the Element of Air

The Fool is the unnumbered card and, like the Joker in a conventional pack of cards, can occur anywhere, and even replace any of the other cards. The Fool is the spirit of chaos, of the unexpected. It is also a card of innocence and the simple joy of living.

Astrologically the card is governed by the Airy element, which makes it as free as the wind. Also, the planet Uranus, which is considered the most eccentric of the planets, ensures that the card is quite lawless, original and inventive.

Meaning: Nothing can harm you, whatever you do! Take a risk. The start of a new chapter in life. Expect the unexpected. Unconventional people could enter your life.

Reversed meaning: Folly, madness. Look before you leap!

THE MAGICIAN

Card I
Ruled by Mercury

The Magician

This figure represents a travelling entertainer and showman, a common enough character in medieval Europe. Part mountebank, part wise man, and possibly also a pickpocket, the Magician lived on the fringes of the law and was regarded with a mixture of fascination and suspicion by both the authorities and the people. Whenever he appears in the cards you can be sure that the old adage of 'The quickness of the hand deceives the eye' is coming into play!

The Magician is always number one – at centre stage and in the spotlight. This apparent forthrightness is misleading, because there is always something going on behind the scenes.

The image exudes originality and confidence. The card is associated with positive action, individuality and creativity.

Meaning: Generally, the card shows new beginnings, the start of a new cycle, a sense of purpose, willpower and initiative. The Magician is a card of potential showing the importance of a new enterprise.

Reversed meaning: Trickery and deception are the negative face of the Magician. Be careful in whom you place your trust.

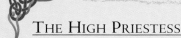

THE HIGH PRIESTESS

Card II
Ruled by the Moon

The High Priestess, or Female Pope, is shown as a wise woman dressed in blue robes reminiscent of the Virgin Mary or of a nun. In many traditional decks she wears the triple crown similar to that of

The High Priestess

the Hierophant (card 5), but here she wears the horned crown of the goddess Isis.

She holds a scroll marked 'Tora' and sits between two pillars representing severity and mercy. Her robes are patterned with pomegranates suggesting the mystery of life and death. It is also a symbol of virginity, and so by implication of the virgin Moon goddess who sheds the morning dew, according to ancient belief.

Meaning: When the High Priestess appears in the cards a secret is about to be revealed. Often the card shows a strong feminine influence, and in a man's reading it can represent the most important woman in his life. The card shows mystic power, psychic ability and the unconscious mind. It relates to memory and intuition. Rely on instincts.

Reversed meaning: Delay all plans, because there are hidden obstacles or enemies. Be discreet.

THE EMPRESS

Card III
Ruled by Venus

The Empress is the third numbered card in the Major Arcana. The number three is indicative of synthesis and harmony, childbirth and maternal productivity. The Empress is shown as an earth mother, fertile and caring, surrounded by comfort and abundance. Her crown is surmounted by twelve stars representing the signs of the zodiac. She has been called 'the star-crowned empress, herself the morning star'. This is a direct identification with the goddess Venus, 'the morning star', who, apart from her more usual realm of love, is also a deity associated with fruitfulness and harvest.

Meaning: This card points to abundance, material and domestic comfort, security and protection. It is obviously a maternal card so may indicate childbirth, motherhood, nurturing, reassurance and a firm foundation for future progress. The card is associated with springtime.

Reversed meaning: Being over-protective and tyrannical, emotional blackmail and perhaps poverty. Possibly problems in pregnancy.

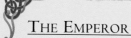

THE EMPEROR

Card IV
Ruled by Aries

The Emperor, a regal man in middle age, exudes confidence and accomplishment. Crowned and dressed in ornate robes, he surveys a barren domain. At his feet is a shield bearing the device of an imperial eagle, symbol of worldly power and aspiration.

The arms of his throne are decorated with ram's heads, and the Emperor holds a sceptre with a ram's head. These symbols relate to the astrological sign of Aries, which governs the card.

Only one side of the face is seen. This suggests that the Emperor is only concerned with one side of life. In a woman's reading this card can show an important man with paternal overtones.

Meaning: High honour, the achievement of ambition. It may show an influential man whose help may be required. It is the card of bosses and people in authority. The Emperor represents the man in control in any given situation or problem. To a woman, he may represent her husband or father.

Reversed meaning: Tyrannical attitudes and the abuse of power. Ambitions unfulfilled and a craving for status.

THE HIEROPHANT, HIGH PRIEST OR POPE

Card V
Ruled by Taurus

The Hierophant

The Hierophant, or Pope, is the male counterpart of the High Priestess (card II). But whereas she is concerned with intuitive wisdom, the Hierophant is more connected with concept of moral law. The title of the card originates from Ancient Greece and merely means 'Priest'. This card, like the Emperor, is connected with fatherhood. This time, though, the power is not worldly but spiritual. The triple cross and three-tiered crown featured in the card represent the divine, intellectual and physical worlds. In Christian terms they show the trinity of Father, Son and Holy Spirit.

Meaning: The Hierophant symbolizes a wise and capable advisor, forgiveness and comfort, the influence of established faith and the power of the conscious mind. The Hierophant could represent a teacher and rules to get along by. The cards following could offer advice.

Reversed meaning: Bad advice, bewilderment and confusion. A crisis of faith and disorderly conduct. More positively, making one's own rules without reference to what has gone before.

THE LOVERS

Card VI
Ruled by Gemini

This card obviously refers to strong emotions, a choice of the heart that cannot be made by logic alone. In older packs this card often showed a young man who had to make a decision between two women while Cupid hovered above, aiming his dart.

Later versions of the card replaced Cupid with the fiery archangel St Michael, and the group below by figures of Adam and Eve complete with the Trees of Knowledge and of Life. However, hidden in one of them is the serpent of temptation.

The card represents the power of the human heart, the power of attraction and a need to listen to one's desires and a deep emotional nature.

Meaning: A decisive point has been reached. An important choice must be made with reference to true desires rather than duty. A dramatic change of attitude will lead to happier times. Love, reconciliation and physical pleasures. A happy relationship in personal life or in business.

Reversed meaning: An unhappy love affair, a failure to make up one's mind, unwelcome separation and emotional loss.

THE CHARIOT

Card VII
Ruled by Cancer

VII

The Chariot

A crowned conqueror stands erect in a chariot that has four columns and a luxuriant canopy. The chariot is drawn by two sphinxes symbolizing the mystery of the future as well as the positive and negative forces that draw us through our lives.

There is an obvious similarity between this card and the Ancient Roman triumphal processions in which a general would parade through Rome at the head of his victorious legions. There is one word of warning implied here though. A slave would stand behind the conqueror whispering, 'Look not so proud for the gods are jealous.' In other words it is vital not to become so flushed with success as to become arrogant, as some Roman emperors found to their cost.

Meaning: Victory, conquest over difficult odds. The force of destiny which drives one to achieve great things. Travel, movement generally, renewed optimism and motivation. Be self-reliant and you will gain success. Also unexpected good news.

Reversed meaning: Being out of control, arrogance and bad temper. Travel plans that go wrong. Temporary delays and frustration.

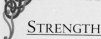

STRENGTH

Card VIII
Ruled by Leo

The Strength card shows a woman in the act of opening a lion's mouth. To attempt such a thing is obviously indicative of courage and fortitude, especially since the lady is wearing no protection. However, this is an act she accomplishes with gentle firmness, leaving the lion in no doubt as to her determination.

The card is governed by the sign of Leo, indicating honour, reliability, honesty and a fixed sense of purpose.

This card is a good indication of recovery from illness or other difficulties. It may describe a situation that must be reacted to bravely even though you are afraid. Resolute action and a willingness to stand up for what is right no matter what the consequences are shown by the card.

Meaning: Physical strength, courage defeating mean attitudes and hatred. You will triumph over your enemies. If ill health has been experienced, then rapid improvement will occur. A fight for fair play.

Reversed meaning: Cowardice, loss of nerve. Giving in, or being beaten by unfair means. You must overcome your own fears.

THE HERMIT

Card IX
Ruled by Virgo

IX

The Hermit

An old bearded man in a monk's habit holds up a lamp to light his way in the darkness. He leans upon a staff. The mood of the card is one of loneliness and fear of the dark, each footstep must be placed with care, for the Hermit does not know his way.

The card points to re-evaluation. The Hermit is an old man who looks back on his past and realizes that there must be more than this. He knows next to nothing of the greater reality and fears his own ignorance. However, the Hermit does show a willingness to remedy that ignorance and gives the patience and descipline required to utilize past experiences and old lessons to make the most out of the future.

Meaning: The card may stand for caution, patience, old age and experience. A prudent attitude is advised, so sudden courses of action are not the wisest at this time. A realization that there is always something new to learn. This is a warning against thoughtless actions.

Reversed meaning: Impatience, loneliness and obstinacy. Do not disregard advice from older and wiser folk.

THE WHEEL OF FORTUNE

Card X
Ruled by Jupiter

The Wheel of Fortune

The Wheel of Fortune was a medieval symbol of the vanity of man and of earthly power. It is found as far back as Ancient Greece as the spinning wheel of three goddesses known as the Fates. There may be a hint of this in 'The Sleeping Beauty', the story of the three fairies and the fateful curse, concerning a spinning wheel, that they impose on an infant princess.

Traditional sayings associated with the card are concerned with the beasts and with the wheel itself. The Sphinx at the top says 'I rule', the serpent 'I have ruled', and the dog 'I will rule'. The wheel itself is 'Without rule', since the power of the Fates exceeded that of the gods themselves.

When the wheel is reversed the meaning of the saying 'Life is a lottery' becomes very obvious indeed.

Meaning: A 'turn for the better', the end result of past actions and the workings of destiny, which no one can completely understand. An end to current problems and some marked strokes of luck.

Reversed meaning: Bad luck and unpleasant surprises. Remember that the wheel will turn in your favour eventually.

JUSTICE

Card XI
Ruled by Libra

The crowned figure of Justice is often seen seated between pillars representing mercy and punishment. In her hands she holds the balance and sword. Her face is resolute and firm in conviction. She wears no blindfold, so she sees all the facts, and does not permit temptation or envy to misguide her.

The Justice card suggests the ignorance of the law is no more excuse in the courts of life than it is in the courts of men. Laws must be studied and obeyed if the penalties for transgressing them are to be avoided. However, being too harsh is also a mistake; the balance must not be tipped. Although the human judicial system may be fooled, divine justice can never be escaped.

Meaning: Good judgement, success in all legal affairs. A decision will go your way. Signing of contracts, unity, balance and harmony. The righting of a wrong. An advantageous business proposal.

Reversed meaning: Injustice, bad judgement and decisions going against you. Legal matters will not go well. Misguided advice.

Justice

THE HANGED MAN

Card XII
Ruled by Neptune and
the Watery Element

XII

The Hanged Man

The Hanged Man is one of the strangest cards in the Tarot. A man hanging upside down from a branch or scaffold, who doesn't actually seem to mind. The key to the figure lies in the man's expression, which is of pleasure, exactly the opposite of what one would expect. This is the central theme of the card – a reversal of the expected.

The card's ruler, Neptune, is a planet associated with self-sacrifice, dreams, inspiration and mysticism. Its watery nature shows that time is fluid and dissolves all prejudices and preconceptions eventually.

Meaning: A temporary pause in life. Go with the flow and accept the changes that are occurring. Cultivate patience. Perhaps you have to sacrifice something so something greater can be gained. Rarely, the Hanged Man can mean illness. You may feel that you are walking a tightrope for a while because events around you will make you feel very uncertain.

Reversed meaning: Selfishness is holding you back. Manipulation, especially emotional blackmail. Perhaps you are playing the martyr.

DEATH

Card XIII
Ruled by Scorpio

The image here is the common one of the Grim Reaper; riding a white horse, he steps over the bodies of men, commoners, princes and bishops alike – none are excepted. This is the skull face of fate at its harshest to which all humanity is subject. In many Tarot card decks Death is depicted wearing a full suit of armour.

The symbol of Death as an armed warrior is taken from the Book of Revelation, Chapter 5: 'Behold a pale horse, and his name that sat on him was death, and hell followed after him.' The skeleton symbolism shows that the inner self (the skeleton) is the most durable part of the physical self.

Meaning: Transformation, change which is a blessing in disguise. A clearing out which will make way for something better. Harsh fate which does not consider personal feelings. Very, very occasionally does the card signify death; more usually it means a major change in life.

Reversed meaning: An enforced change, a removal of something that should have been given up. The loss of a friendship.

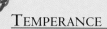

TEMPERANCE

Card XIV
Ruled by Sagittarius

A winged angelic figure is pouring liquid from a cup or pitcher in her left hand to a cup in her right. This represents the flow of the unseen and mysterious into the seen and known, or from the unconscious mind to the conscious.

The card relates to mixture. In old alchemy it was seen as the doctrine of solution in which all elements are combined. The angel possesses wings yet stands on earth and water while her halo is of fire. The angelic figure itself is of uncertain gender, as indeed are all angels.

Meaning: Careful control of volatile factors resulting in a successful conclusion. A harmonious partnership, peace restored after a troubled time. Self-control and adaptability. The power of imagination being such that wishes can be fulfilled.

Reversed meaning: Quarrels, competing interests, unfortunate combinations of events and people. Corruption and domestic strife.

XIV

Temperance

THE DEVIL

Card XV
Ruled by Capricorn

The image of the Devil is a familiar if sinister one. In the Tarot he squats above two slavish familiars who are chained to his pedestal.

This is the card of materialism at its worst. The Devil rules the tyranny of the physical body and senses. The Devil is the bearer of the inevitable, often of disaster and misery; it is connected with lust and greed, and with a refusal to recognize anything other than the value of pleasure for its own sake.

Meaning: Unyielding power, tyranny, lust and greed. An immovable obstacle that cannot be overcome yet may be worked around. Discontent and depression caused by an overwhelming force. It also means unbreakable bonds, so, strangely, it is a good omen for marriage!

Reversed meaning: The beginning of freedom, light at the end of the tunnel, the overcoming of bad habits and addictions. Charitable deeds and thoughts.

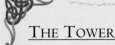

THE TOWER

Card XVI
Ruled by Mars

A sturdy tower erected on a hill is struck by lightning. The castellated top of the tower is lifted by the blast and fire strikes deep within. Flames roar from three narrow windows as two figures fall from their ruined refuge.

The Tower is a symbol of safety. In this case, of course, it was not so safe after all. Too much trust had been placed in its thick walls by the builders and those who lived within. The windows denote a narrow view of the world. The card reflects the fact that nothing can stand against the will of the divine.

Meaning: The breaking down of an outworn sense of values. A sudden shock that is nevertheless a blessing in disguise. Freedom from old, possibly self-imposed restrictions. Sudden disruptive change is inevitable but nothing to be feared, since you will come through this experience a better and stronger person.

Reversed meaning: False accusations, imprisonment and oppression. Another interpretation is that you will cause a sudden change or show a rebellious attitude that will be a shock, surprise or dismay to others.

THE STAR

Card XVII
Ruled by Aquarius

This card is one of the more mysterious images of the Tarot. A naked maiden pours water from two pitchers. One stream flows into a pool, the other on to dry land. Above her, eight stars shine brightly, while a bird perches in a tree in the background.

The idea of wishing upon a star is at the centre of the card's meaning. It shows that the universe is not the senseless, unjust place that it can seem to be. The Star card shows that there is always something else, even when the going is really tough. The card can show a gesture of affection, perhaps a gift. Remember that the gifts of the Star are not always material.

Meaning: Insight, understanding and hope for the future. This card is a good indication that wishes will be fulfilled, not always as one expects, but even so, the unexpected can have a good result. The Star shows good health and that gifts will be given. The spiritual dimension of life should not be ignored.

Reversed meaning: Tension, pessimism, obstinacy and lack of opportunity. Bright hopes seem to have been dashed.

THE MOON

Card XVIII
Ruled by Pisces

The dark landscape beneath the Moon is full of threats. The lobster or crayfish in the pool in the foreground symbolizes the primitive mind rising towards the light. Two beasts, usually identified as a dog and a wolf, stand before two towers. The wolf symbolizes wildness and animal instincts, while the dog represents domesticity and mundane life. Both of these are a trap; the truth lies between them on the rocky road that leads over the horizon under the watchful gaze of the mysterious Moon.

Meaning: Take care, for all is not as it seems. You need to use your intuition to deal with a deceptive situation. The path you are on is difficult and may cause fear, but continue along it, even if you are beset by doubts, because all will eventually turn out well. This card is favourable if you are involved in a clandestine love affair.

Reversed meaning: Unforeseen perils, lies and terrible risks. Be very careful indeed. Hidden enemies lurk and you will have to keep your wits about you if you are to defeat their wiles.

XVIII

The Moon

The mood of the card is buoyant and happy. The glorious Sun bestows the gift of life to all the universe. The child, without saddle or bridle, represents the perfect control between the conscious and unconscious mind. The child's nakedness shows that he has nothing to hide. The sunflowers symbolize the four elements of Earth, Air, Fire and Water.

Meaning: Success, glory, happiness, joy and achievement. Happy reunions and joyful love affairs. Pleasure, vitality and good health. The Sun card can signify summer or hot sunny places. Children are also shown by this card, perhaps good news concerning offspring, or a longed-for baby will be born.

Reversed meaning: The Sun card cannot be too negative – perhaps there will be some delays in achieving the full joy of the Sun. Possibly there will be some minor setbacks on the way.

THE SUN

Card XIX
Ruled by the Sun

A beaming sun gazes down on a naked child riding a white horse. The child holds up a banner. Behind him is a wall, over which sunflowers are seen, or the sunflowers may be shown on open ground.

JUDGEMENT

Card XX
Ruled by Pluto and
the Fire Element

A conventional Christian scene of the last Judgement is seen in this card. The Fiery archangel Michael sounds the last trumpet and the dead rise from their graves to be judged on their conduct in life.

The main concern of the card is death and rebirth. The symbolism, though Christian here, is a familiar kind found in many cultures such as Persian, Norse, Hindu and ancient Greek mythology as well as in modern Voodoo. It can signify far-reaching decisions that cannot be reneged upon.

Meaning: New potential. An opportunity which, once given, must not be ignored! The call to fresh efforts. A new project and a decision that will affect the rest of your life. Career success and the enjoyment of past efforts. This card speeds up the pace of the rest of the cards and shows that the outcome will be quicker than you expect.

Reversed meaning:
Opportunities ignored, fear, and a refusal to move from your position. Fear of death and illness. Refusal to change when change is vital. Reversed, Judgement delays outcomes.

Judgement

THE WORLD

Card XXI
Ruled by Saturn

As we reach the World card, the cycle begun by the Fool is completed. A dancer clothed only in a scarf dances within a wreath. In the corners of the card are seen four figures of a man, a bull, a lion and an eagle, representing first, the four elements; secondly, the four fixed signs of the zodiac, Aquarius, Taurus, Leo and Scorpio (here, Scorpio is shown as its alternative symbol of an eagle); and thirdly, the Four evangelists Matthew, Mark, Luke and John. They may also represent the four cardinal directions, the four winds, etc.

The semi-clad dancer seems female, but it is claimed that it is in fact hermaphrodite, having characteristics of both sexes and thus reconciling all opposites.

Meaning: The completion of any task. The rewards of labour and success. Triumph in all your undertakings. The end of one cycle and the start of another. This is considered the best card in the pack, showing that battles are over and triumph is yours.

Reversed meaning: Success is yet to be won. Perhaps your own insecurity stands in the way of completion. Too great an attachment to what is at the expense of what could be. You may be lacking in vision.

The Minor Arcana

THE SUIT OF WANDS

The suit of Wands, which in an ordinary deck of cards are Clubs, are also known in the Tarot as Staves, Rods or Batons. Traditionally the suit relates to the element of Fire and is associated with growth, creativity, work and enterprise. It is a masculine suit and often shows the influence of the Fire signs of the zodiac: Aries, Leo and Sagittarius.

THE ACE OF WANDS

Keyword: Enterprise

Meaning: All aces indicate beginnings, as far as the ace of Wands is concerned this is the beginning of enterprise. If this card occurs, an important new business or relationship is indicated.

Reversed meaning: Restlessness, an uncontrolled desire for change for its own sake. Lack of confidence and a need for the support of others.

The Two of Wands

Keyword: Partnership

Meaning: A successful and prosperous partnership is often shown by the appearance of the Two of Wands. A meeting of minds will enhance projects and lead to success. Think more positively about your prospects.

Reversed meaning: A clash of personalities or friction within an established partnership. Success that leaves you unsatisfied.

The Three of Wands

Keyword: Opportunity

Meaning: The Three of Wands is a card of luck, showing that your ship will soon come in and that your current worries will soon be resolved. You may need just a little more patience, but you can be assured that your troubles will soon be at an end.

Reversed meaning: Pride, arrogance and a refusal to appreciate the truth could be hampering your efforts. Stubborn independence.

The Four of Wands

Keyword: Prosperity

Meaning: The Four of Wands is the card of harvest. It means the successful conclusion of a project. It can show personal achievement and material well-being. Apart from that, it is a card of the home and may show improvements to a property or that a move is imminent.

Reversed meaning: Restriction and a feeling of pointlessness. Ingratitude or disappointment. Unfulfilled hopes cause regret.

THE FIVE OF WANDS

Keyword: Challenge

Meaning: An exciting challenge which raises the adrenaline. Competitions; a need to prove oneself. Sporting interests could now be stimulated. The card also indicates a good time to hold negotiations concerning business.

Reversed meaning: Quarrels and misunderstandings. Legal affairs cause worry and there is the danger of far-reaching deception.

THE SIX OF WANDS

Keyword: Victory

Meaning: A major ambition will be fulfilled. Success is foretold in any venture. You may have to work for it, but you will achieve a greater victory than you expect. Be bold and daring, because audacity is bound to pay off at this time.

Reversed meaning: Anxiety, success delayed, fear for the future – however, the prospects are still good, even though you may worry about them.

THE SEVEN OF WANDS

Keyword: Defiance

Meaning: This card shows a time of adversity when it is important to stand your ground and not give an inch! Be stubborn and stand up for yourself, because only a firm attitude and resolute actions will win the day. You will eventually triumph over great odds.

Reversed meaning: Timidity, self-doubt and indecision at the worst possible time. Believe in yourself, otherwise defeat is certain.

THE EIGHT OF WANDS

Keyword: Swiftness

Meaning: The end of delays, travel, movement and swift resolution of problems. Communications of all kinds, phone calls, letters and many journeys. Understanding and co-operation, helpful companions. Good news is on its way.

Reversed meaning: Delays, unexpected hitches in travel plans. Impetuous or premature actions. Exhaustion. This is not a time to put your views in writing. Envy.

THE NINE OF WANDS

Keyword: Resilience

Meaning: Self-confidence, stability and strength. In times of stress the appearance of this card is reassuring, promising that you have all you need to maintain your position and eventually prosper. Patience is a virtue. Remain vigilant.

Reversed meaning: Obstinacy, a refusal to compromise in any way, an unbending will, fixed and erroneous attitudes.

THE TEN OF WANDS

Keyword: Burden

Meaning: Heavy duties, and a stressful and hard-working life. Burdens may be shouldered on behalf of others. Difficult tasks to complete; however, you will successfully complete your work, even though the price in terms of health and anxiety may be high. Perhaps some obligations have to go.

Reversed meaning: You may be taken advantage of; subversion, hidden enemies. Attempts will be made to disrupt your plans.

THE PAGE OF WANDS

Physical description: A fair or brown-haired youngster with blue or hazel eyes.

Meaning: A traveller. An adaptable, hard-working and enthusiastic young person with an impulsive nature. A messenger. The Page of Wands may be hyperactive with little staying power and easily bored.

Reversed meaning: A complainer who likes his or her own way. A faithless lover. A bringer of bad news. There may be reading or writing problems.

THE KNIGHT OF WANDS

Physical description: A robust young man with a ruddy complexion.

Meaning: An energetic warrior, a generous friend or a lover. He has a hasty personality and is quick to love or hate. This Knight can also mean a change of home.

Reversed meaning: A jealous person who thrives on conflict. An argumentative and aggressive man.

THE QUEEN OF WANDS

Physical description: A dignified woman of fiery temperament. She is likely to be fair with blue or hazel eyes.

Meaning: A freedom-loving woman who is lively, active and creatively gifted. She may run a business or hold a responsible position. She is warm-natured and a practical organizer of others. A lover of nature.

Reversed meaning: A possessive woman who hates independence in others. Bad-tempered and dictatorial. A jealous and vengeful woman.

THE KING OF WANDS

Physical description: A mature man of authority. He is much travelled and worldly wise. His hair is probably brown, his eyes blue or hazel.

Meaning: An athletic man, strong and healthy. Honourable in an old-fashioned sense, he may be a businessman. He is just, kind and generous. He makes an excellent advisor. He is sexually passionate.

Reversed meaning: An intolerant, bigoted man, possibly violent and belligerent. A bad advisor who is governed by his passions.

THE SUIT OF CUPS

The Cup cards are associated with emotions. In a more ordinary deck these are the 'Hearts'. The Cups are ruled by the watery element and are associated with the astrological signs of Cancer, Scorpio and Pisces. A majority of Cups in a reading shows that the main issue is one of love.

THE ACE OF CUPS

Keyword: Love

Meaning: The start of love, inspired creativity that is nurtured by fruitfulness and happy times. Artistic excellence, a love affair, marriage, betrothal or a birth. All affairs of the heart will prosper.

Reversed meaning: Bitterness, exhaustion, despair, the loss of faith in love and disenchantment within a relationship. A love affair could be coming to an end. Emotional stress or unreal expectations of love.

The Two of Cups

Keyword: Commitment

Meaning: Love and understanding between two people. Harmonious relations and emotional contentment. It may show that, in this case, opposites attract. When the link is not deeply emotional, it can show co-operation, mutual respect, friendship and the ending of rivalry.

Reversed meaning: Divorce, separation, possibly temporary. Infidelity, betrayal and disappointment.

The Three of Cups

Keyword: Celebrations

Meaning: Happiness and reunions. Parties and meetings which lead to love affairs and lots of flirtation. In some cases this card can indicate pregnancy or birth. Ills are healed and harmony achieved. Attendance at weddings or christenings is likely.

Reversed meaning: Taking others' feelings for granted. Unbridled passion and promiscuity. The 'eternal triangle' in love affairs. Perhaps affection not returned.

The Four of Cups

Keyword: Boredom

Meaning: Having reached stability within a relationship, what more can be achieved? This could be a case of familiarity breeding contempt. There needs to be a new start to renew the spark in an old relationship. New interests, activities and friends are required.

Reversed meaning: Fear of loneliness, and over-indulgence in physical pleasures in order to stave off boredom. Often depression leads to abuse of alcohol.

THE FIVE OF CUPS

Keyword: Sorrow

Meaning: Loss of a relationship, sorrow, emotional hurt and feeling of worthlessness. However, although the card seems to be grim, the outlook is good and urges you to stop crying over spilt milk and look in another direction for happiness.

Reversed meaning: Difficult circumstances, yet you will gain more than you have lost. An unhappy time will soon end.

THE SIX OF CUPS

Keyword: Memory

Meaning: Strong links to the past, perhaps an old friend or lover will turn up soon. Childhood, past efforts are about to be rewarded. The answer to a specific question lies in a similar situation in the past. Possibly a move of home nearer to your point of origin.

Reversed meaning: Nostalgia, the inability to accept change or adapt to new conditions. Bad memories and old, unresolved pain.

THE SEVEN OF CUPS

Keyword: Choices

Meaning: An important decision has to be made; however, there are many options to choose from. Make your decision carefully, since all is not as it seems. Doorways of opportunity open, but you have to develop intuition to know which one to go through.

Reversed meaning: False hope, the loss of opportunity through wrong decision-making or inaction. Emotional fantasies.

THE EIGHT OF CUPS

Keyword: Seeking
Meaning: Don't be afraid to leave the past behind.
Travel. There is plenty more in the world to see and
experience. If you are disillusioned with your life
now, take heart, because the future promises to be
brighter. Follow your heart and do what you truly
desire.
Reversed meaning: Running away from problems.
Abandonment of what is good and secure in pursuit
of an impossible dream.

THE NINE OF CUPS

Keyword: Pleasure
Meaning: Excellent social life, parties, good friends and
fun. Places where people meet. Good health,
happiness and popularity. Relationships will be very
fulfilling. Ease of communication and the flow of new
ideas.
Reversed meaning: Vanity, complacency, overly
sentimental attitudes and carelessness. A partner
may feel neglected.

THE TEN OF CUPS

Keyword: Contentment
Meaning: Peace, friendship, good companionship and
family happiness that is going to last. An excellent
card for group activities denoting success and fun. It
foretells a wish fulfilled and that everything will work
out for the best.
Reversed meaning: Mistrust and rivalries in a previously
happy situation. Losing touch with friends and
relatives. Feelings of isolation and misunderstanding.

Page

Cups

THE PAGE OF CUPS

Physical description: Pale, with fair hair and blue eyes.

Meaning: A young person or one with a youthful cast of mind, gentle and loving, artistic and insightful. If a girl, somewhat tomboyish, if a boy, then somewhat feminine. This person could be emotionally vulnerable and needs affection.

Reversed meaning: A trivial and spoilt person, one who manipulates others' feelings. Perhaps this person lives in a dream world.

Knight

Cups

THE KNIGHT OF CUPS

Physical description: A young man, often well travelled with a fair complexion, casual in appearance.

Meaning: A faithful lover or good friend, enthusiastic, passionate and amiable. He brings offers and opportunities. The Knight is often poetic and graceful.

Reversed meaning: An idle swindler, a false lover who is a heart-breaker. Possibly the card shows a lover going away.

THE QUEEN OF CUPS

Physical description: A beautiful woman, with expressive eyes and sensuous lips. Her hair colouring is generally fair.

Meaning: A warm, sympathetic and sociable woman. She may be artistically gifted and very imaginative. The Queen is honest, loyal and devoted to those she loves.

Reversed meaning: A vain and immoral woman, who is deceitful and perverse. Someone who constantly demands attention.

THE KING OF CUPS

Physical description: A mature man who has achieved something in life. Usually with a good complexion and clear, liquid eyes.

Meaning: A sociable, loving, sensuous man who has intelligence combined with a strong intuition. Warm-hearted and loyal, he enjoys the comforts of life and has a love of the arts. His attitude is responsible and generous.

Reversed meaning: A crafty and possibly hot-tempered man. He gives a misleading impression. 'Still waters run deep.' He is very secretive and yet may be easily hurt.

THE SUIT OF SWORDS

The Sword cards are known as Spades (from the Italian for Sword) in a conventional deck of cards. The Suit relates to the element of Air and is associated with mental activity, strife and troubles. The suit is masculine and often shows the influence of the astrological signs of Gemini, Libra and Aquarius.

THE ACE OF SWORDS

Keyword: Force

Meaning: The Ace of Swords shows the start of an unstoppable movement. Things are changing for the good. Success is guaranteed, as the card cuts through all obstacles. As with all Sword cards, the Ace shows that there are battles to be fought, but with courage and intellect, nothing can stand in your way for long.

Reversed meaning: Injustice, wanton abuse of power, misunderstandings and malice. Mental stress and anxiety.

THE TWO OF SWORDS

Keyword: Balance

Meaning: Friendship at a time of adversity. An ally upon whom you can depend. A decision has to be made logically, but there are no clues as to which direction to take. A balance between two equally matched opponents. A duel, either literally or one fought with words.

Reversed meaning: Malicious stirring up of trouble. Betrayal by someone you trust, trickery and fraud. Your own indecision may be to blame.

THE THREE OF SWORDS

Keyword: Heartache

Meaning: A painful ending of a relationship. That which has stood in your way is now being removed. Possibly a three-way relationship in which heartache is inevitable for one participant or all. Minor surgery is possible.

Reversed meaning: Confusion and worry, a great upheaval that causes stress. The healing process has begun, even though you have a long way to go.

THE FOUR OF SWORDS

Keyword: Recuperation

Meaning: A need to retreat from the troubles of life. The opportunity to rest and to put your thoughts in order. A peaceful interlude during which strategies can be worked out. Visits to hospitals but not necessarily a personal illness.

Reversed meaning: Illness, exile or confinement. Gloomy thoughts and depressive attitudes. Nervous exhaustion enforcing rest.

THE FIVE OF SWORDS

Keyword: Defeat
Meaning: Failure and loss. Defeat in battle, a conflict will go against you. Cut your losses and swallow your pride. You may have to back-track and start again. The course you are on will bring nothing but misery. You must accept that a change of direction is necessary.
Reversed meaning: Stubborn pride and a refusal to give in, even when all is lost. Attendance at a funeral is a traditional interpretation.

THE SIX OF SWORDS

Keyword: Travel
Meaning: Movement away from danger. Discretion being the better part of valour! Travel in company, being with others in the same circumstances. Immediate problems will be solved. A positive direction to go in.
Reversed meaning: Delays and petty problems, partial success and an inability to see where you are going.

THE SEVEN OF SWORDS

Keyword: Dishonesty
Meaning: Direct confrontation to an opponent will not work. You have to be cunning and use all your wiles to defeat an enemy. Perhaps you have to sacrifice something in order to succeed. Your efforts may not be whole-hearted.
Reversed meaning: Theft, lies and malice. Look after your possessions and do not give your trust too readily.

THE EIGHT OF SWORDS

Keyword: Restriction
Meaning: A run of bad luck, feelings of being trapped and powerless. Patient effort is needed to get out of this difficult situation. Help is available if you can forget pride and ask for it. Restrictions will gradually fade.
Reversed meaning: Frustration, which you take out on others. Being your own worst enemy, placing restrictions upon yourself.

THE NINE OF SWORDS

Keyword: Cruelty
Meaning: Anxiety and sleepless nights, spite and slander which undermine confidence. Suffering that is for eventual good such as putting up with painful treatment in order to get better. Female health problems and, possibly, self-punishment and guilt.
Reversed meaning: A refusal to accept help or even feel that improvements are possible. However, there is light at the end of the tunnel.

THE TEN OF SWORDS

Keyword: Ruin
Meaning: This is the worst card in the pack. Betrayed, lost, cold and loveless this card shows the lowest point in fortune. However, since this is the worst it can get, improvements must surely follow. The only way from here is up!
Reversed meaning: A troubled time which will go on for a while yet. Don't give in to negative thinking or you will ruin your own prospects.

Page

Swords

THE PAGE OF SWORDS

Physical description: A dark-haired youngster with deep penetrating eyes.

Meaning: A quick-witted and intelligent youngster, eloquent and sharp. Eager to learn and adept at turning situations to his or her advantage. The Page may bring news, contacts and gossip.

Reversed meaning: A spy, rival or slanderer. A spiteful person who lies for his or her own ends.

THE KNIGHT OF SWORDS

Physical description: A tall, dark-haired young man with a lot of charm and wit.

Meaning: An eloquent and confident person who is fast-moving and easily bored. He can be impetuous and is the type who breezes into one's life and then just as swiftly breezes out again. A good ally with subtle reasoning powers.

Reversed meaning: A quarrelsome and possibly violent person, secretive and treacherous. Apparently honest, he is actually a liar.

Knight

Swords

The Queen of Swords

Physical description: A mature woman, possibly a widow or divorcee.

Meaning: An independent lady, she is intelligent, rational and tends to be cool in a crisis. Graceful, possibly with a fondness for music and dancing. She is very alert to undercurrents and should not be underestimated.

Reversed meaning: A bitter, malicious and jealous woman. Possibly a prude, she is a harsh judge of other people's morals and actions.

The King of Swords

Physical description: A mature man with dark hair and eyes, possibly a lawyer, doctor or other professional advisor.

Meaning: An intelligent man in a position of trust and authority. He is a wise and loyal advisor. Logical and calm, he dislikes overt displays of emotion. He requires a lot of mental stimulation.

Reversed meaning: A distrustful, suspicious person, one who intrigues and plays mind games. A double dealer or con man.

THE SUIT OF PENTACLES

The Pentacles cards are also called Coins or Discs. In a conventional deck these are the Diamonds. The suit relates to the element of Earth and is associated with money, prosperity and land. It is a feminine suit and often shows the influence of the earth signs of the zodiac: Taurus, Virgo and Capricorn.

Ace

Pentacles

THE ACE OF PENTACLES

Keyword: Foundation
Meaning: This card shows the beginnings of prosperity. It provides a firm foundation upon which to build. Security, stability and financial improvements. Possibly a windfall or a monetary gain through gambling.
Reversed meaning: Greed, insecurity and financial worries. Unsound investments and stupid speculation.

THE TWO OF PENTACLES

Keyword: Juggling

Meaning: Hard times, but you will cope. Income equals
expenditure but the finances are still coming in and
you will still be solvent. An exercise in intelligence
dedicated to improving a difficult situation. A cash-
flow crisis. Spreading resources thinly.

Reversed meaning: Reckless attitudes to money and
security. Unwise gambling, possibly resulting in
bankruptcy.

THE THREE OF PENTACLES

Keyword: Skill

Meaning: The use of skills and talents in order to make
a profit. High achievement, rising above friends and
opponents equally. Possibly being the subject of envy
from those who are less talented. Sometimes a move
of house.

Reversed meaning: A waste of talent. Attitudes that are
too conservative, or a refusal to take a risk.

THE FOUR OF PENTACLES

Keyword: Possessions

Meaning: Material stability and holding on to the
security and possessions you have gained. Financial
problems will be overcome and you will find yourself
in a comfortable situation. Money in the bank.

Reversed meaning: Miserly attitudes, a grasping
mentality. Avarice, discontent and envy of others.

THE FIVE OF PENTACLES

Keyword: Poverty

Meaning: Monetary loss, hardship. You will not be alone in this misfortune because others will share in this fate; however, all is not lost, and fresh opportunities await to be found. You may be looking for financial or emotional support in the wrong place.

Reversed meaning: Bankruptcy or other great loss which could have been avoided. A rapid change of attitude to money is now needed.

THE SIX OF PENTACLES

Keyword: Generosity

Meaning: Money put to good use. Help from someone else, charity, gifts and benevolence. Do not waste this bounty but put it to good use. Someone sees hidden talents in you. Financial support. Outstanding debts will be paid.

Reversed meaning: Money flowing out like water. The squandering of resources. Careless loss of possessions.

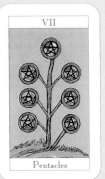

THE SEVEN OF PENTACLES

Keyword: Planning

Meaning: Slow growth and forward planning. Long-term plans will come to fruition eventually, but much patient effort is needed. Hard work, yet you may feel that you are going nowhere fast, but that is not the case. Be persistent.

Reversed meaning: Idleness, wasted efforts and discouragement.

THE EIGHT OF PENTACLES

Keyword: Learning

Meaning: The development of new skills, patient effort towards a long-term goal. The addition to one's education, the gaining of qualifications. The skills you learn now will eventually be turned to profitable ends. Work now for future rewards. A new job.

Reversed meaning: Impatience, a desire for quick success at the expense of reputation and quality. The loss of a job.

THE NINE OF PENTACLES

Keyword: Comfort

Meaning: Enjoyment of the comfort that money can buy. Prosperity, good sense and financial shrewdness. This card relates to good administration of resources and shows that relaxation is now possible after hard work. The purchase of new furniture and a connection with gardens.

Reversed meaning: Heavy debts, or a successful life that rests on the misfortunes of others. Danger of theft.

THE TEN OF PENTACLES

Keyword: Wealth

Meaning: Wealth, success and honour. A good family life, and excellent relations between generations. Inheritance and family property. This card can also be an indicator of marriage and the carrying on of a family tradition.

Reversed meaning: Hidebound tradition stifling new thought. Problems of inheritance and family disputes over money.

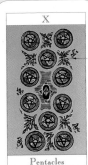

Page

Pentacles

THE PAGE OF PENTACLES

Physical description: An introverted boy or girl with black hair and eyes and a swarthy or tanned complexion.

Meaning: A conscientious person, thrifty and capable. Someone who has little money but splendid prospects. A student with a sense of duty. A patient person. Also there may be good news about money.

Reversed meaning: A wastrel, a dissolute and impatient person who has a constant need for money. A scrounger.

THE KNIGHT OF PENTACLES

Physical description: A swarthy or earthy young man with very dark hair and eyes.

Meaning: A conventional, practical young man who leaves nothing to chance. The Knight accepts responsibility easily and is no stranger to hard work. He is trustworthy and steadfast.

Reversed meaning: A boring, static personality with little imagination. Dull, timid, smug and careless.

Knight

Pentacles

THE QUEEN OF PENTACLES

Physical description: A large, motherly woman with a strong constitution and cheerful demeanour. Her colouring is dark.

Meaning: A sensible, matronly woman who has a good head for business. Kind-hearted and charitable, she also has a taste for luxury. Sometimes moody, her general personality is very caring.

Reversed meaning: A possessive and miserly woman who hates change, possibly a harlot. A suspicious, mistrustful person.

THE KING OF PENTACLES

Physical description: A dark man who holds considerable responsibility.

Meaning: A practical realist. A businessman, bank manager or farmer who has considerable wealth. He is generally married and is very shrewd. Despite his wealth he is unpretentious. He has a stable personality and is slow to anger.

Reversed meaning: A stupid, unimaginative man who is easily bribed. Associates with gamblers. He is a bad enemy to make.

Combinations of Cards

Sometimes groups of cards crop up in a reading, and these groupings have special interpretations of their own. The closer the cards are together, the greater their influence.

ACES

Four: A time of beginnings. Lots of energy and potential.

Three: Good news is on its way.

Two: Partnership. A new home or love affair.

TWOS

Four: Gatherings of people.

Three: Many changes.

THREES

Four: Creativity, determination.
Three: Deceit, changeable circumstances.

FOURS

Four: Contentment, security.
Three: Hard work ahead.

FIVES

Four: Competition, discord.
Three: Routine activities, stability.

SIXES

Four: Good fellowship and harmony.
Three: Achievements.

SEVENS

Four: Intrigue, lies and theft.
Three: Good fortune.
Two: True love.

EIGHTS

Four: Journeys and news.
Three: Good news about
   relationships.
Two: Surprises.

NINES

Four: High achievements and
   rewards.
Three: Good health and prosperity.
Two: Legal documents and contracts.

TENS

Four: Remarkable triumph (if any
   are reversed then obstacles to
   overcome).
Three: Legal problems.
Two: New employment and good
   luck.

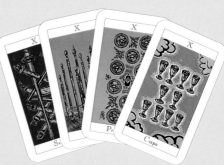

PAGES

Four: Schools, colleges, universities, groups of young people.

Three: Good social life, fun, lively parties.

Two: Quarrels between friends.

KNIGHTS

Four: Speedy action.

Three: Small gatherings of men.

Two: Reunions with old friends.

QUEENS

Four: Small gatherings of women (if cards reversed, may be spoiled).

Three: Helpful female friends.

Two: Gossip, rivalry and back-stabbing.

KINGS

Four: High achievements. Important affairs. Recognition by peers.

Three: Powerful and influential men.

Two: Business partnership, co-operation.

Reading the Cards

CAN I READ MY OWN CARDS?

I have often been asked whether it is unlucky to read your own cards. The answer to that question is undoubtedly no! However, it is rare that you will get a fully revealing answer to a question or even that you will understand it, even if the cards are as clear as day. It is only when reading for another person that the full subtlety of Tarot reading come into its own. Also, this is the best way to learn.

HOW TO BEGIN

First, clear your mind of all extraneous thoughts. Shuffle the cards (remembering to reverse some) while considering the issues you want to know about. If you find it helps, speak your question out loud, and when you feel that you have shuffled enough, begin to lay out the cards.

If reading for someone else, go through the same procedure, allowing the enquirer to shuffle and to voice his or her own question.

TAROT SPREADS

There are many patterns into which the cards are laid out to create a reading. These patterns, called 'spreads', can be general or specific. If general, no question is asked and the reader gains an overall impression of the enquirer's life and the events which will shape it in the future. The more specific type of reading requires a direct question to be asked by the enquirer while shuffling the cards.

Apprentice Tarot readers often have difficulty in reading a lot of cards at once, so the examples included in this book start with the simpler spreads for you to practise on before you move on to the more complex general patterns.

THE THREE-CARD SPREAD

This must be the simplest of all Tarot spreads. It involves laying out three cards to represent past, present and future.
Example: The three cards are the Nine of Swords, Temperance and the Sun. This indicates that in the past there was a lot of anxiety, probably due to a bad mixture of people. In the present, Temperance reveals that the situation is becoming more harmonious and many of the problems are fading away. The Sun card in the future shows that there is a lot of happiness in store — maybe a love affair or a holiday in a warm country.

THE CROSS SPREAD

The Cross spread is a little more complex, involving six cards. Follow the shuffling procedure and lay out five cards in the shape of a cross, starting at the bottom as in the illustration. Then put one card aside. This will be the overall result card. The Cross spread is very good for answering specific questions.

Card 1 = The past and the influence the past still has on your question.
Card 2 = Obstacles in your path.
Card 3 = Influences working in your favour.

Card 4 = The near future.
Card 5 = The long-term future.
Card 6 = The eventual outcome in your life.

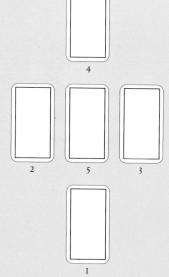

THE HORSESHOE SPREAD

The Horseshoe spread has seven cards and is very adaptable. It is good for general readings and for answering specific questions.

Card 1 = The past.
Card 2 = The present.
Card 3 = Hidden influences at work.
Card 4 = Obstacles to be overcome.

Card 5 = The attitudes of other people.
Card 6 = What you should do.
Card 7 = The outcome.

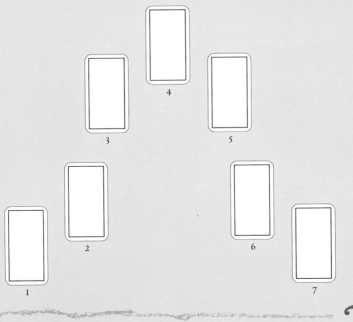

THE FAN SPREAD

This spread is a little more advanced and is suitable for a general reading in which no question is necessary. The first step is to select a card that represents the person you are reading for. Usually this will be a Court Card of the Minor Arcana. Shuffle and lay out the cards in seven groups of three.

Group 1 = The character of the enquirer and the recent past.
Group 2 = Love life and emotional links.
Group 3 = What the enquirer desires.

Group 4 = What the enquirer expects.
Group 5 = The unexpected or unknown factors.
Group 6 = The near future.
Group 7 = The distant future.

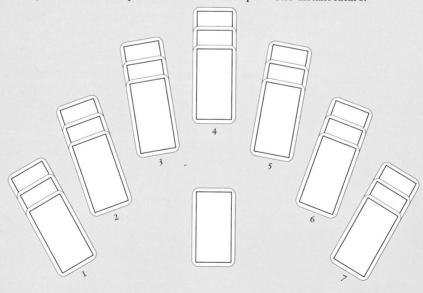

THE CALENDAR SPREAD

Here, thirteen cards are laid out with one in the centre and a
further twelve in a circle around it. This spread is excellent for
timing events and for foretelling the enquirer's fortunes throughout
the twelve months following the month in which the
reading is done.

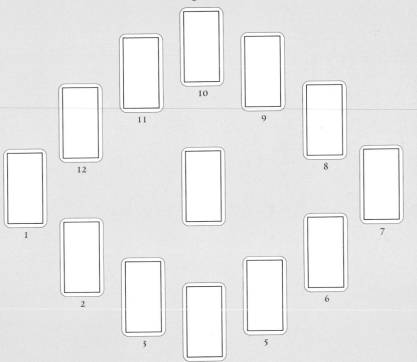

THE HOROSCOPE SPREAD

The Calendar spread can also be adapted into the Horoscope Spread, in which each of the cards represents an area of the enquirer's life. If you use this option, decide first whether you are using this spread as a calendar or as a horoscope.

Centre card = General influences on the enquirer.

Card 1 = Personality of enquirer.

Card 2 = Money, possessions and material concerns.

Card 3 = Short journeys, brothers and sisters, learning.

Card 4 = Home life, childhood.

Card 5 = Romance, leisure, fun and children.

Card 6 = Work, habits and health matters.

Card 7 = Partnerships of all kinds, either business or personal.

Card 8 = Sexuality, shared resources, inheritance and investments.

Card 9 = Distant travels, religion and philosophy.

Card 10 = Career, status and direction.

Card 11 = Friends, social life and hopes for the future.

Card 12 = Secrets, hidden enemies and where you are your own worst enemy.

Timing with the Cards

Apart from the 'Calendar' methods of laying out the cards, there are also ways of timing an event using the cards of the Minor Arcana. This is especially true when specific questions have been asked.

First, count backwards from the last card that you have laid down. Ignore all Major Arcana cards and Court cards, then take note of the suit and the number of the first Minor numbered card that you come to.

In this system, each suit corresponds to a different measurement of time:

Cups = days (but cannot be counted unless next to a Pentacle card)
Wands = weeks
Swords = months
Pentacles = years

So if the last card placed in a reading was the Six of Wands, the events spoken of in the interpretation would occur within six weeks.

At the risk of confusing you, I should point out that individual cards often have a time period associated with them. The Moon often refers to one lunar cycle of twenty-eight days. The Sun could refer to summer, the Empress to spring, and the Star to Christmas, as well as the astrological signs associated with various Major Arcana cards.

The Minor Arcana suits, too, often refer to seasons. Wands are associated with springtime, Cups with summer, Pentacles with autumn and Swords with the sharp cold of winter.

Further Reading

If you are interested in taking your knowledge of the Tarot cards a step further, I can heartily recommend the following books on the subject. All the cards used in these books are various Tarot decks, but the rules remain the same whichever Tarot is used. Happy Tarot Reading!

Fenton, Sasha: *Fortune Telling by Tarot Cards* (Aquarian Press)
Fenton, Sasha: *The Tarot in Action* (Aquarian Press)
Fenton, Sasha: *Super Tarot* (Aquarian Press)
Lyle, Jane: *Tarot* (Hamlyn)